What Mushers Are Saying About *Husky Song* ....

Husky Song puts into words many of the hard-to-describe, wonderful aspects of running sled dogs. Shannon captures innermost feelings that exist in the magical bond of sled dogs and their human companions. Her writing truly describes many of the almost mystical feelings I have experienced in the past ten years of running these beautiful, faithful, amazing animals."
— *Larry LeMaster, M.D.*
John Beargrease 190
Sled Dog Race champion

"[Patsy Shannon's] book once again made me appreciate the time, place and special opportunities given me. The cold, the snow and that special canine connection. Well done. Everyone who's lived it will appreciate this book. Those who only dream it will drive harder to achieve it.
— *Marlo Larson*
Sled dog driver

Patsy Shannon's narratives are a tribute to sled dogs everywhere and to the special relationship this musher has with her huskies. Reading the verses, you feel the wonder and enjoyment as though you were right there on the trail with Patsy and her dogs. It's a special book about special times.
—*Jack Welsh, musher*
Iditarod Sled Dog Race official

I.S.B.N. 0-911007-43-1

Ryan Press
Route 2, Box 206B
Lake Park, Minnesota 56554

Husky Song

Patsy Shannon

Photographs by Dan Knudsen

*To my family
and to all of the dogs
who have been my friends*

Table of Contents

Whisper on the Wind

there's a whisper on the wind
leaves dance upon the grass
the days are growing shorter
as time falls in the hourglass

the huskies are full of Summer fat
unspent energy lies in wait
they sense the time is coming
when they will race out through that gate

today, I brought the sled outside
and in the crisp and sunshine air
I ritualized the preparing
and replaced the worn with rehearsed care

hungry eyes watched me as I worked
with a wanting only they could know
desire of a consummate fury
with inertia the formidable foe

this is the time that we embrace
when huskies sing their mournful song
of trails they so want to run
and of an Autumn far too long

Colors

colors upon the rising moon
tell us we'll be out there soon
running through the trackless snow
joyous in our go

sweetness in the windswept air
a taste of what is lying there
beyond tomorrow, behind the trees
when Autumn air begins to freeze

the dogs dream in September sun
of winding trails they will run
I close my eyes and feel the wind
and imagine snowflakes on my skin

November

new, glistening patches of frosty white
covered the ground during the night
the huskies awoke me with a song of delight
they knew it wouldn't be long now

as my boots crunched across the dusted lawn
eyes sought mine through the air of the dawn
I saw the fresh tracks of a brave doe and a fawn
and I dreamed of the trails of huskies

The Trail Awaits

I draw a breath
my heart beats fast
to see the snow
fall on the grass

the huskies howl
a throaty din
instincts arise
within their skin

I move outside
it is our fate
to meet the night
the trail awaits

Taking Off

the dogs are all on fire
their hearts burn with desire
as they try to jump into the harness

they drag me to the traces
blood pumping, my heart races
as we rush to meet the snowy far-ness

as a magic wand is twirled
silence falls upon our world
the only sound is of paws upon the white

the woods whisper as they lure
us towards the spruce and fir
soon we've disappeared into the moonlit night

Freedom

a cold, cold Winter's night
the air is still, the stars are bright
the moon is full, our spirits light
we travel in the dark

we are at home, the dogs, the sled
while others rest snug in their beds
we steal freedom and we're fed
adventure on the run

they take me where they want to go
onto new trails, fresh carved in snow
by other teams who also know
the freedom of the trails

Not a Sacrifice

she balks at paying full price
for the parka with the ruff
she figures last year's holey one
will be good enough

that afternoon, she writes a check
for several hundred bucks
and thinks nothing of it
as she loads the dog food in the truck

last Winter's boots will be fixed
for duct tape does it all
that vet bill really must be paid
that stood since late last Fall

and that old truck, well it might just last
for another little while
but the booties and the harnesses
can't go another mile

sometimes she thinks it's quite a joke
she eats beans most every day
but she knows it's true, she wouldn't do
it any other way

The Eyes

arctic eyes hold a knowing
pools of wild silence
hazel rings of blue and brown
secrets of defiance

instincts foreign to a man
of nature and its teachings
the dogs hold these through all time
while man falters in his reaching

the smell of an impending storm
of rotten, cloudy ice
readings through the pads of black
will saves a musher's life

fire and ice shine within
the windows of the wise
images of ancient trails
run through husky eyes

The Sentinels

on a night alone out on the trail
deep snow shrouds the sound
of runners as they crease the snow
that lies on frozen ground

the trail curves and we move through
some tall and stately pines
that's dressed in cloaks of sparkling white
the sentinels of time

years ago, men passed here
trappers and the like
the tall trees watched them as they passed
into the lonely night

and those who thirsted for the gold
that lay within these hills
they traveled through these frozen woods
when these were seedlings still

the trees have stood throughout the time
a shelter for the teams
who have passed this way for many years
onward toward their dreams

Sleepless Nights

on this night of blackened cold supreme
the feeling is one as in a dream
the movement hypnotic, the trot of the team
lulls my softened senses

the trail is one that we know well
yet the night holds a mysterious spell
perhaps sleep waits beyond that hill
rest waits upon the weary

I'm tired and dreary, yet filled with joy
though the smallest disturbance proves to annoy
the woods are inviting and seem so coy
we can't afford to trust it

we move along at a relaxed pace
at times, I forget we are in a race
I haven't seen another's face
for miles and miles and miles

so we continue on in our cocoon
our world, the snow, the stars, the moon
I want it to end, but not too soon
ache swims within my bones

Yeller

that dog never asked for much
just a kind word, a gentle touch
she never barked to hook her up
she just watched you with her eyes

her eyes followed me as I'd go
anywhere in the dog yard, I'd always know
she'd wait patiently 'till I reached her row
then she stood completely still

as I'd reach to scratch underneath her chin
she knew the time was soon to begin
she trembled as she helped her legs in
the harness that made her go

now, Yeller is old, older than most
but to any dog musher, I'll offer a toast
she's honest and true, 'tis not a boast
she runs with all she is

but recent years have not been kind
you see, Yeller's still a pup in her mind
but her legs and lungs have not aged like wine
the pups are running up to her

her neck line started to stretch a year back
her tugline once tight, there came a slack
she ended her last two races in the sack
I knew her pride was hurting

today, as I walked out to the lot
her eyes pierced through me like a shot
she was asking a question that I'd hoped she would not
I turned to walk back in

I reached for one that I knew would fit
and walked on over to her to sit
she watched me for a little bit
then she nudged the weathered harness

so then I thought — oh what the hell
the retired row should go for a spell
we'll all feel younger, not over the hill
and I reached for a few of her buddies

and over the hills we ran like the wind
well, not that fast, but I had to grin
if it was a race, we'd surely not win
it didn't seem to matter

I'll still hook her up until she tells me no more
I've got a long way to go to settle the score
faithful and true, right to the core
she runs with all she is

so, here's to Yeller and all of the crew
all the sled dogs that run for me and you
there's rare a friend so trusting and true
as the dogs that run the trails

The Ice

that night
the lake ice quietly waited
weakened by the warm air
unusual this time of year

as they left to run the trail
fog rolled in and slowly
they slipped into the white
wet and warm

the headlight searched the milky funnel
anxiously, he looked
for the others' sled marks
the marks that were his friends

the ice waited
patiently, unforgiving
and then into the blue black
they fell

the musher's headlight
was seen by a man onshore
for a moment
then he saw it no more

morning found the fog lifting
to uncover what the waters
had claimed
for its own

two lead dogs all alone now
wandered aimlessly around the hole
wet and harnessed still, tuglines cut
and they waited for their next command

Into the Night

the molasses sun is slipping beyond the hills
a soft breeze touches my brow
my feet rest upon the runners
the day is now a memory

I hear the soft sound of the sled
as it slips over the crystal snow
creaking and groaning
in protest against the cold

the huskies run without urging
the rhythm is of their own choosing
and it is in this way
that we travel into the night

Toklat

see that old dog out there
the one who stands alone
with his head held high, he watches us
he's the best I've ever known

scars upon his craggy face
marks he wears with pride
arthritis fills his weary bones
a stiffness he can't hide

he's taken me on many miles
leading dogs long since dead
training younger ones to lead
the trails he once led

he's forgotten more than I'll ever know
about running trails, about where to go
when we are cold and far from home
and the wind begins to blow

he's patient when I stroke his head
wags his crooked tail
he tolerates the stillness
but his heart is on the trail

I still take him on shorter runs
the younger ones soon know
that despite the slowing of his gait
he knows just where to go

I fear this Winter's his last one
so I take the extra time
and tell him what a dog he was
when he was in his prime

sometimes I look into his eyes
and wonder if he dreams
of all the trails that he's run
and the ones he'll never see

out in the dog yard yearlings howl
but I hear one special tone
and I turn to watch him sing his song
for Toklat stands alone

Boundary Waters

they say the temperature reads forty-one below
we must move on, down the trail, this is all we know
we are heading home and have a long, long way to go
up in the land they call the Boundary Waters

the lakes up North are wide and long and we are all alone
ice cracks and pops, my wooden sled sounds as if to moan
and add some eerie music to a soundless Winter tone
up in this land where silence lives again

we are all full of stories, ready to be told
of the fish we caught, of the land, still and cold
of the portages where we all slipped, slid and rolled
on the ice beneath the newly fallen snow

long, long nights spent by a fire's warming glow
where the tales of the trails just seemed to grow and grow
how the dogs ran swift and silent as if they came to know
we were traveling in a very special place

on lakes where moose trot across with ease
and wolves watch us from behind the sheltered trees
fish swim beneath the hushed and blue white freeze
at times, we stopped to hear the quiet

now we're heading home and as if to shut the door
the land bids it's good-bye with a cold and savage roar
a storm is coming, so we move to make the shore
knowing we'll be back again

The warm place

I feel the wind upon my face
the sunshine leaves my shoulder
I smell the fragrance of the pines
and the cold as it grows colder

husky fur feels soft and thick
my hand lingers in the warm
as I change the leaders just in time
to meet the coming storm

Under the Spell

they say the dogs have got her
the snow, the trees, the night
at times she thinks of nothing else
but running through the white

she leaves the placid certainty
warmth of a dancing fire
to answer a call, she knows the voice well
a call that speaks of desire

trails untraveled beckon her
on a night of twenty below
the huskies move when they hear her step
and jump to be chosen to go

the unyielding wind bites and claws
more deadly than a beast
but her dogs are good and the woman, strong
the sport is like a feast

she tastes the cold, drinks in the night
the dogs are hungry to go
and like someone who's not eaten for days
the musher devours the show

the stars, the moon, the glistening snow
the hills hold unclaimed treasure
she watches the dogs move in unison
it gives her simple pleasure

yes, they say the dogs have got her
and they want to know just why
she'd like to explain, but quickly refrains
'cause she couldn't if she tried

Sitka

why do you keep her
they often ask
well, I admit
it's quite a task

she's hard to keep
she loves to fight
but her tugline's
always tight

They Claim the Night

late in the sun-warmed afternoon
as shadows dance across our track
we travel with the rising moon
toward the night, toward the black

the huskies seem to know this time
when we return unto the fold
while men retreat and lock their doors
the dogs escape into the cold

now they run as in years past
the stars, the moon, their light
instinctively they are as one
in stealth, they claim the night

The Storm

still, still, the day is still
we travel without sound
not a whisper on the wind
the sun is going down

cold, crisp, the Winter air
bites my cheeks and chin
I pull my mask to cover up
yet the air keeps seeping in

as the shadows melt into the night
the dogs pick up their pace
this is their favorite time I know
and they begin to race

this route is one we all know well
we've traveled many a day
the dogs are swift and confident
home lies two miles away

then, as we leave the evergreens
beyond the sheltered woods
a sudden breeze blows our way
I pull up my parka hood

slowly, slowly, snowflakes drift
upon the swirling ground
the wind is picking up now
my heart beats at the sound

the dogs begin to disappear
in a strange and misty fog
at times, I see them not at all
as we work to make our lodge

I hear my voice call to them
yet I sound so far away
we've only a little way to go
as night replaces day

the trail has blown away from us
I strain to see the route
I halt my dogs many times
to try to make it out

Red and Togo lead the way
I hope they'll feel the trail
beneath the snow drifted ground
I trust they will not fail

the landmarks fade, I try to gauge
our speed and where we are
the icy snow clogs my eyes
I know we can't be far

the dogs have slowed to a trot
their outlines ebb and flow
as if they're ghosts flying o'er
a landscape far below

and, then, beneath the runners
I feel familiar ground
could it be the road outside my home
that we have finally found?

then, we're stopped outside the barn
I see now the yellowed light
a warm and welcome beacon
in a cold and stormy night

and still, still, the dogs stand still
silent in their rest
then, I reach to stroke each of them
with a solemn thankfulness

Red

watching Red, I saw
how her shoulder dipped
so I put her in the sled bag
a lonesome trip

she whined and whimpered softly
for I think she knew
this is where she'd stay
and she didn't like the view

she rode some miles in the sled
unhappy, filled with woe
consoling her would do no good
her pain was in her soul

The Mail Carrier

the long, cool shadows cast
upon the lake, a looking glass
I wind my way through birch and ash
the night a windless quiet

I sense something and look about
I hear a call, some kind of shout
but there is not another on this route
the moon hangs full and bright

they say this trail was once the one
a man called Beargrease mushed upon
with huskies bred and born to run
they brought the Northern mail

then, the wind picks up, a gentle breeze
I hear a rustling in the trees
a whisper of a haw or gee
I stop my dogs to listen

but the night is quiet and full of black
so I turn my dogs to head on back
perhaps that musher still travels this track
his spirit carried on the Northern winds

The Moose

it was at night, in the pale moon light
that I grabbed the driving bow
and hung on tight, for all my might
and tried to not let go

for they'd seen the moose and it cooked my goose
'cause she had with her a calf
if I'd not been scared, I would have stared
and let out a little laugh

a moose is a sight, in the pale moon light
with the legs so long and strange
with the droopy ears, and the nose appears
like a bulbous, weird-shaped thing

but she can be mean and the instincts keen
for she hates a dog team so
'cause they lurch and leap across the deep
to charge the worthy foe

I stepped on the brake for our own life's sake
and yelled for them to whoa
but their ears were perked and they quickly jerked
us across the punchy snow

I couldn't think because in a wink
we had reached that massive moose
she stood her ground and without a sound
laid out that hangman's noose

her head went low, o'er the blue-tinged snow
the moon made her eyes seem yellow
she froze and stared, my soul laid bare
when she let out a chilling bellow

the dogs leaped and nipped and swerved and dipped
to avoid the deadly hit
by hooves so fierce, they could quickly pierce
a skull with just one kick

I had no gun, never needed one
but how I wished I'd had
for it looked as though in the azure snow
that it might end up quite bad

so I grabbed an ax that I always packed
to clear a brushy trail
and I charged that moose, my nerves hung loose
my arms began to flail

my aim was not to mark or maim,
this mother and her babe
I hoped no red would be shed
and we'd all be on our way

I swerved and swayed and tried to stay
clear of the deadly strike
I heard the yelps, I had to help
but I didn't want the fight

I yelled, I screamed, I sounded mean
I hoped I'd look quite strange
and the moose would see, and maybe flee
from someone quite deranged

the blade shown bright in the moon's own light
as I swung it to and fro
it sliced the air, the metal bare
lit the dark with a strange, weird glow

I swung it higher, as though on fire,
I swung with all my might
it cast a beam, a metallic stream
a crazy kind of sight

before I knew, the moose soon flew
unscathed, with her calf in tow
and I stood there wet, bathed in my sweat
in the moon's half-milky glow

and I stayed and stared at the wondrous glare
to wait for my heart to slow
then I reached to grasp the gleaming ax
from the still and cold blue snow

Fun

softness lies within the silence
on a moonless Winter night
freedom whispers from the woods
to come dance in the white

so I harness up the huskies
and we run off in the trees
a child's game of fun reframed
laughter warms the Arctic freeze

The Trapper

he poured a little whiskey
into an old tin cup
raised his drink up in the air
before he drank'r up

here's to you, my trusted friends
we've had ourselves a day
tomorrow might bring better luck
but, today you've earned your pay

the dogs around the campfire
looked up an seemed to listen
they turned their heads, their ears were perked
his eyes began to glisten

for they knew the ritual so well,
his words were not for them,
yet they sat there quiet and let him go
for years they've been good friends

this could have been a scene right from
a pub or cramped saloon
instead of huskies and a man
under a Winter's moon

the whiskey jumped upon his tongue
found that familiar hold
and he spoke of what he always did
and that was one word-gold

he mumbled, then he cursed the world
that brought him such bad luck
the dogs heads lowered at his tone
then he drained the second cup

he had sold all that he ever owned
to give it all a whirl
and maybe strike it rich some day
and find himself a girl

but that day never dawned for him
and the picture seemed to fray
as years piled on top of years
his youth just slipped away

and now he sits out on the trail
and runs an old trap line
the price of furs ain't what it was
back in a kinder time

and the dogs all listen, watch and wait
for the man to fall asleep
then they turn on back and curl up tight
in the snow that lies so deep

Husky Song

slipping slowly beyond the hills
the sun bids its good-bye
the huskies greet the coming night
and emit a mournful cry

one single song starts silky low
and breaks the still, crisp air
the others join, one by one
and blend a song beyond compare

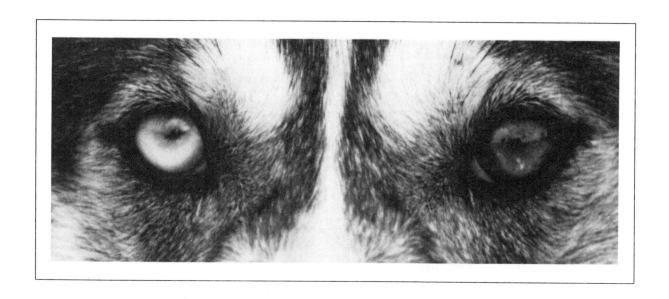

That Dog

oh that dog will never get it
he does not have the drive
just lopes along, with tail up
he makes me want to sigh

I said this to myself one day
on a long and fruitless run
it was as though he didn't care
I'd hoped he'd be "the one"

the one who'd lead me on my way
over trails never wandered
onto perfect runs that warm the heart
into karma never pondered

then, one long night in a race
my leader in the sack
I had no choice, he had to lead
I moved him from the back

and on we went, my spirit sunk
lower every mile
I felt the chance was really lost
and then, I had to smile

I called to him with all the cheer
of a crowd at Notre Dame
I pretended that he was "the one"
and that "leader" was his name

so on and on, we traveled on
I sang him little songs
and told him that he was the best
and that I'd been all wrong

and somewhere on that shadowed route
sometime in the night
that dog that did not have the head
had somehow found the light

and I was humbled by his drive
by the courage that he showed
in the cold and lonely Arctic night
my mind cried out "he knows!"

and now he is the lead dog
the one I hold with trust
by chance I found a precious jewel
a diamond in the rough

Morning

the sun rises slowly
born beneath the ground
warms my face and shoulders
arrives without a sound

the outline of the dogs
intensifies with light
we have broken through to day
from the cold solitude of night

puffs of breath linger
in the still and sun-kissed air
I welcome the coming day
and all that we share

Christmas Eve

my fur mitts know the feel of this bow
my runners know the trail
my huskies know this route so well
that through the cold we sail

I pull the ruff around my face
across the lake there shines a light
the sound of music is faint but true
on this very silent night

Lost Team

I set the hook as best I could
in the thin and crusty snow
and hurried to change the leaders
so we could quickly go

I kept my eyes upon the sled
my hand at ready grasp
quickly worked the snaps and lines
thought we were safe at last

then as I stepped to grasp the bow
my head turned at a sound
a deer running through the woods
the way they leap and bound

a moment's hesitation
a second so misspent
they lurched against their harnesses
hook popped and off they went

at first, I ran and yelled at them
my heavy boots made chase
but they felt the lightness of the sled
and I'd not win this race

I watched the sled go o'er the hill
and then I was alone
sweating in my coveralls
six miles from my home

untroubled by the closing night
unworried by the cold
my thoughts were on my wayward team
the dangers to unfold

a neckline hooked around a tree
a tangle, then a fight
these thoughts kept me running on
through the dark, black night

on, on, I ran on
with a silent prayer
that they were on the trail home
and I would find them there

I followed paw prints faint and light
upon the icy snow
an occasional runner mark
would sometimes barely show

time went by, I walked and ran
the sweat upon my brow
I hoped they might just make it back
that they'd be home by now

I saw the light of my barn
as I came upon the hill
my eyes sought out the shapes
of the team I knew so well

and there, oh there, could it be
them stretched out on the ground
each curled up in a ball
so warm and safe and sound

and when I reached to check each one
and finding nothing wrong
they looked up at me as if to say
and, what took you so long ?

Diamonds

she's fifteen and all she can think about
is diamonds
glittering hues of purple, blue and pink
dancing on a Winter's morning

she's fifteen and all she wants to do
is run her huskies
through the sun-sparkled jewels
on the crystalline blankets of white

The Hawk

a red-tailed hawk glides above
I feel his searching eyes
on my team of black against the white
from his vantage in the sky

I watch him glide in silent circles
and disappear into a field
emerging as this day's victor
with what the earth has to yield

Cabin in the Pines

it's Christmas night and all is still
I look out toward the trees
the quiet places call to us
the air begins to freeze

I clutch a harness in my hand
dogs scramble from their beds
limber up their backs and bones
I load our little sled

a thermos full of hot black joe
banana bread I pack
snacks for all the working dogs
it all goes in the sack

and soon we're off down the trail
to our cabin in the grove
the tiny one room stopping place
with that old potbelly stove

the trail is lightly sprinkled white
with new fresh fallen snow
illuminated by the moon
a reassuring glow

and when we reach our little house
I break out all the cheer
to toast the dogs that pulled the sled
and brought us all to here

they chew their Christmas sausages
then roll upon the snow
bellies full, spirits light
they wait for me to go

I hesitate and look around
and tarry in the time
the moment seems so crystalline
the night air, so sublime

a hushed and private little world
silence cloaks our souls
nestled in the snowy woods
a mother's kind of hold

and far away, we hear the peal
of church bells in the night
the dogs ears perk, they look toward
the sound across the white

one by one, they raise their heads
to celebrate the time
and a joyous song filters from
the cabin in the pines

Hearts of Fire

fibers hewn of blood and grit
the husky heart will never quit
born with knowledge and desire
hearts of gold, hearts of fire

molded strong with the miles
of trails won, of forests wild
of ice that holds impending peril
the nerve is hard, the instincts feral

my heart beats fast, I watch in awe
to see the drive, rough and raw
and watch the paws grip the ground
the rhythm pure of silent sound

the nucleus pumps with red
ancestral lineage is fed
pumping strong with quiet knowing
the destiny is in the going

The Dance

three quarters moon
a silent night
the dogs run sure
the tuglines tight

serene and pure
a rhythmic pace
the trotting paws
a dancer's grace

Tomorrow's Team

these pups have never been this way
they've never run this trail
so I speak to them with trust
to tell them they'll not fail

their ears, they flicker back to me
so I tell them it's all right
and they throw their shoulders to the test
and make their tuglines tight

I watch their backs, their ears and hips
and stop upon a crest
as I look at each of them
their eyes tell me the rest

who is tired and who is not
and who is learning the game
each of them is young and strong
yet none is just the same

but soon they want to go
so I pull the straining hook
they move ahead in unison
without a backward look

further down the sunswept trail
I see a familiar gait
an ear bent just a certain way
or another long ago trait

and my mind returns to years ago
of other trails, other days
when I first ran a team of dogs
and learned of husky ways

those dogs taught me what they knew
I tried to learn it well
those days and dogs meant much to me
much more than I can tell

and as I look at these young ones
I'm filled with a kind of pride
but I can not take the credit
I can only take the ride

and so I call to tomorrow's team
my voice is filled with hope
and as we cross onto the trail home
they break into a lope

The Northern Lights

my boots upon the frozen ground
make that familiar grinding sound
the still night air bites with cold
a timeless chill of Winter's old

the sky is dark and lit with lights
luminescent sparks of white
my huskies curl inside their straw
as mercury falls rough and raw

and I turn North and search the sky
for Winter's visual lullaby
magic flowing from the North
that only nature could bring forth

and there across the blue black sky
sweeping paint strokes swirl on high
dancing ivory ribbons gleam
illuminate a milky stream

my eyes take in the very sight
a tonic for a cold, cold night
pouring forth from heaven's chalice
the Aurora Borealis

Spring

as the stillness of a Winter's night
lies blanket to the hoot owl's call
I listen at the frosted window
hearing time as it falls

today, the winds of April
blew in it's first gentle breeze
in the afternoon's warming sun
they ran with strength and ease

then they curled up in the twilight sun
bellies full and spirits spent
upon patches of warm, brown earth
creatures knowing true content

April

when the days grow longer
the earth begins to thaw
to warm beneath the sun
I'll walk out to the barn

hang the well-worn harnesses
upon that peg
gather up ganglines
haul the sled upstairs

walk out in the shirtsleeve sun
strange upon my white arms
and say good-bye to the season
with much regret and longing

About the Author

Patsy Shannon grew up in Enumclaw, Washington. She graduated from the University of Washington, where she competed as a "Husky" on the UW track team. She moved to Minnesota in 1985 and purchased her first sled dog. In 1990, she began competing in sled dog races in the Upper Midwest. In addition to her interest in mushing, Shannon works as a family counselor, writes cowboy poetry and runs marathons.

Photographer: Dan Knudsen, Advanced Images Photography, Fargo, North Dakota